Pop Pop's Train Ride

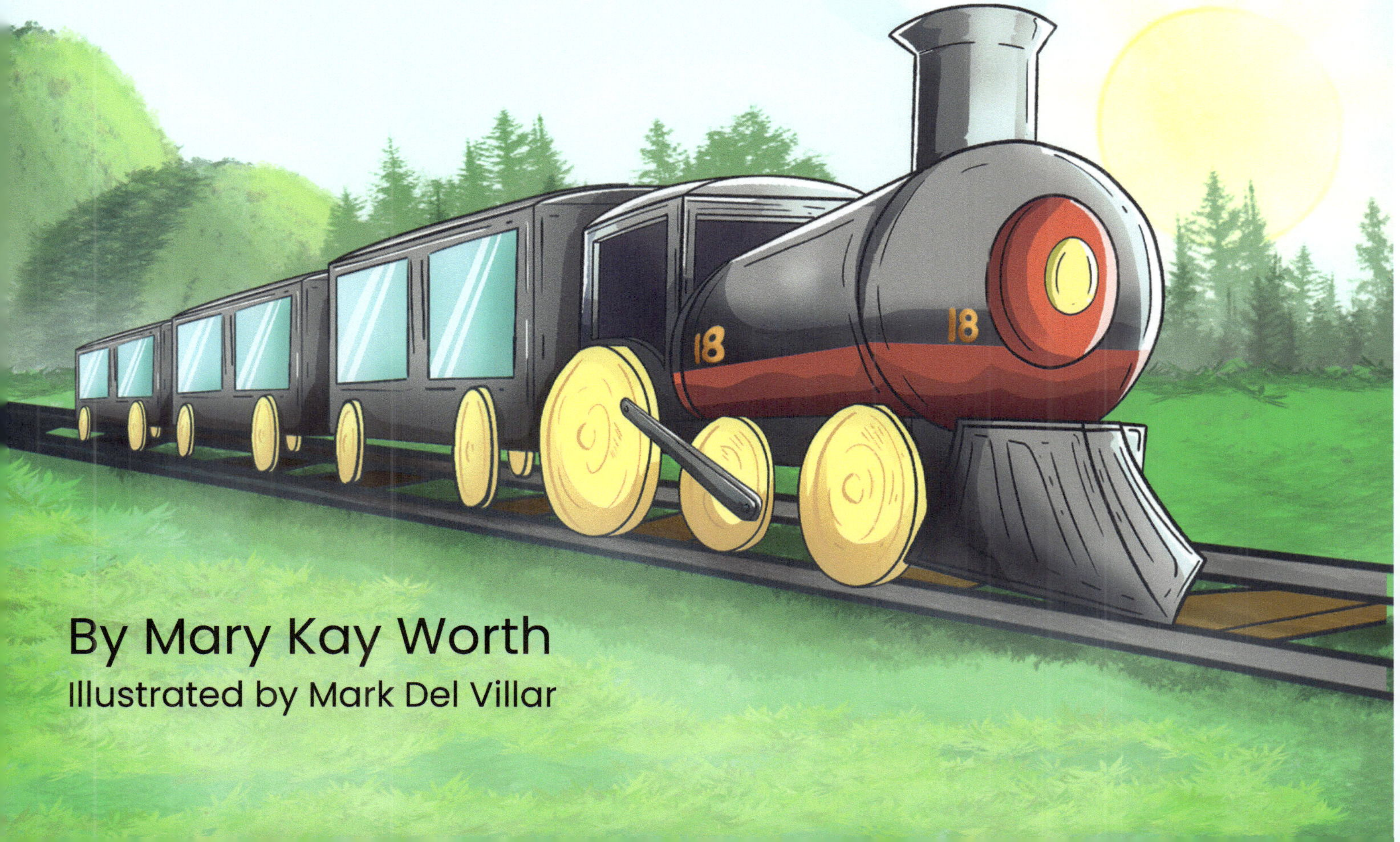

By Mary Kay Worth

Illustrated by Mark Del Villar

Ordering Information:
You may search this book in Amazon, Barnes & Nobles and other online retailers by searching using the ISBN below.

ISBN (eBook):   978-1-956742-47-3
ISBN (Paperback):   978-1-956742-29-9
ISBN (Hardback):   978-1-956742-49-7

I almost didn't even ask. Then I listened. My Dad, my Pop, joined me for the videotaping. I moved home after retirement to take care of my parents. Pop took care of me. This is for Pop. I love you.

Dedicated to
James "Jim" "Gumps" William Worth in heaven

Let's take a train ride!
Down the tracks!
Pop Pop likes the train.
Clickety-clack!

Tickets! Porter!
We're boarding soon!
Pop Pop's train ride leaves at noon!

Train cars need an engine!
Here it comes!
Chug-a-chug-a CHOO CHOO!
WHOOO WHOOO !

Big black engine! ONE EIGHT
See white steam! Don't be late!

4

Find the bell, whistle, too!
Pop Pop's train ride for all of you!

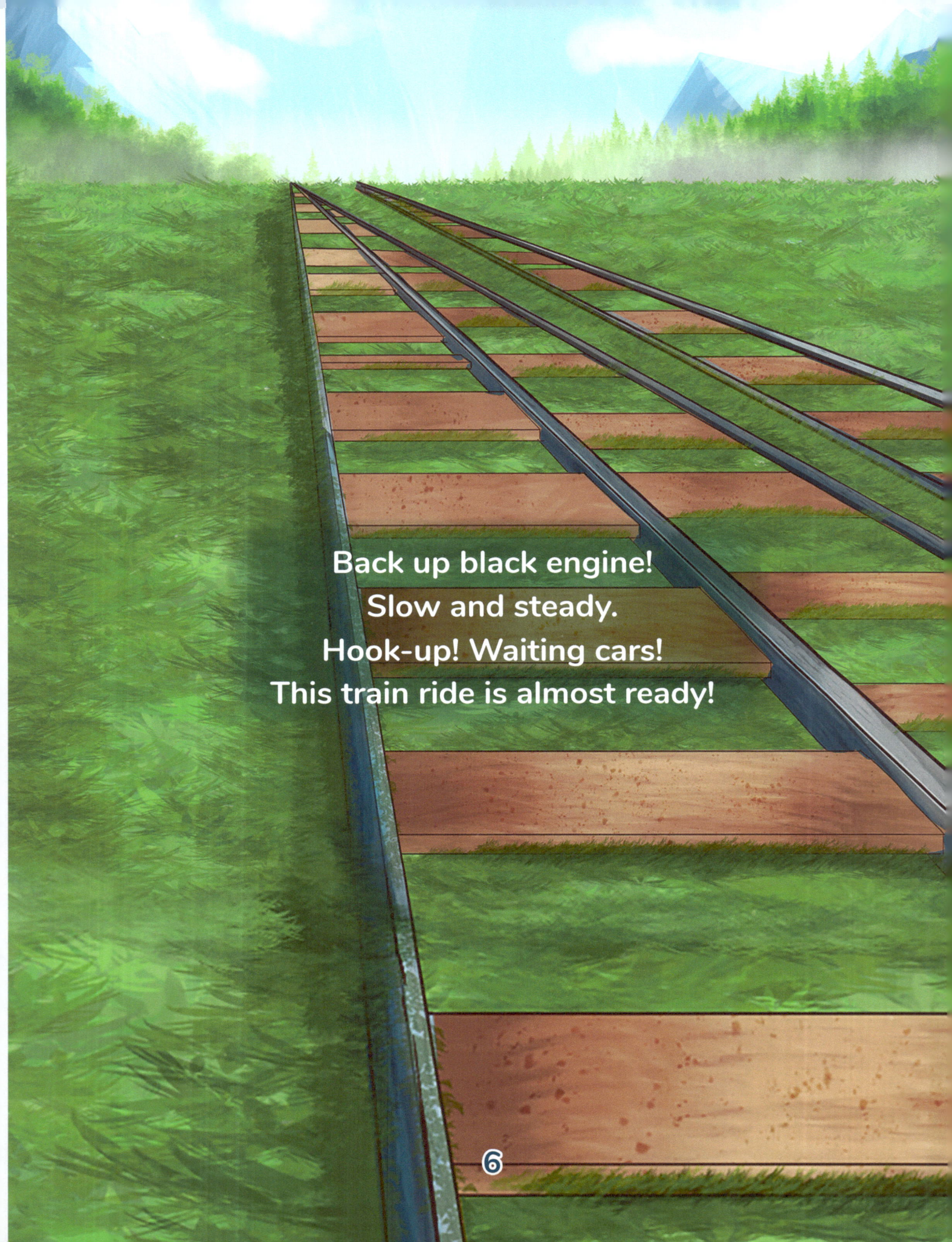

Back up black engine!
Slow and steady.
Hook-up! Waiting cars!
This train ride is almost ready!

6

Steam and smoke. Look! See!
Black soot. YIPPEE!
Red 1 -8; ONE-EIGHT here!
CH-CH-CH-CH-CH-CH-CHEER!

"ALL ABOARD!"
The conductor said.
Up black stairs.
Watch your head!

Find a seat! "Look! Here's one!"
It's about time for lots of fun!

Outside seats are open, too!
Chug-a-chug-a CHOO CHOO !
WHOOO WHOOO !

Pulling out!
Clickety-clack!
Move! Whistle!
Down the track!

11

"Hi!" Happy Pop Pop.
Ball cap on top.
Talk to conductors,
"How do we stop?"

Time for songs about the train!
Down the tracks and back again.

14

Riding the rails. CLAP and SING!
Train whistle now. Hear it RING!

Orange station. Rest stop here.
Move black engine to the rear.

Pull us back now, down the track!

Pop Pop's train ride! Clickety-clack!

Child of God, Grandma, Mother, Daughter, Sister, Friend
Person with Disabilities
Teacher, Principal, Superintendent, Professor
Traveler, Storyteller, Photographer, Actor, Musician, Author, Owner

Mary Kay is a native of Portville, NY, and now lives in Hampton, VA.
Following 30+ years in public education, Mary Kay has nine published
titles: *HEY ELEPHANT! WHERE ARE YOU?* , *Banele – the Girl from
Swaziland*, *Mountains Trees Plant and Flowers of Swaziland*, *Dear Deer*,
The Truth About Santa, *Three Christmas Stories*, *Pop Pop's Train Ride*,
The Great Train Robbery, and *A Lucky Stone Day*. **Available through
Mary Kay's website or Amazon.**
For more information check out Mary Kay's website:
http://www.marykayworthofficial.com .